Made in United States
Orlando, FL
12 August 2022

20914799R00057